TGIT

THANK GOD IT'S TODAY

BARRY GOTTLIEB

ISBN: 1-4392-1000-4
ISBN-13: 9781439210000

Visit www.booksurge.com to order additional copies.

FORWARD

♦ TGIT (tig'-it) is a mantra of gratitude

♦ TGIT is an awareness of the "good", the "positive", and the "best of times" that exists all the time

♦ TGIT is a movement focused on passing the "good" forward

♦ Every day is a gift

♦ The quality of your life is your gift to yourself

♦ YES... You *do* have a choice

Did you know:

♦ The average person has over 10,000 thoughts a day

♦ Recent research estimates that the average American's thoughts are negative almost 80% of the time

♦ Note: Over 80% of media coverage is negative in nature

We can be different:

♦ For the first hour and the last hour of every day:

  o No television

  o No radio

  o No newspaper

Promote the positive...
Read, watch, or listen to:

- ◆ Something inspirational

- ◆ Something educational

- ◆ Something spiritual

- ◆ Start and end your day on a positive note

Affirmations

- ◆ The two most powerful affirmations are:

    - ○ "I like myself"

    - ○ "I am responsible"

- ◆ Recite these affirmations every morning and every evening o Repeat each one, three times

o Say them aloud

o Say them with passion

Role Models

♦ It is time to give our children positive role models to look up to

♦ Look for and share positive stories at dinner

♦ Have your children share their own positive stories at dinner

♦ Focus on the "GOOD"

This book is designed to help you start your day off on a positive note, and to place positive thoughts in your mind at bedtime.

You don't have to read the chapters in order. Just turn to any topic you choose... or open to any page.

The chapters are brief and to the point.

Remember, knowledge is not power until you use it. I hope you will use the information in this book to assist you in reaching your full potential.

The best way to insure learning this useful information is to "pass it forward". When you teach, you become the student.

I TGIT (tig'-it)................. Do you?

Barry Gottlieb

TABLE OF CONTENTS

DEDICATION

To my amazing, wonderful children, Briana and Luke. They are the two greatest gifts a man could ever hope for. They taught me that we are born enlightened.

A note of appreciation and gratitude for all of the incredible mentors that have had such a positive influence on my life: Fred and Dorothy Bishop, Wayne Dyer, Zig Ziglar, Ed Forman, Earl Nightingale, Dr. Denis Waitley, Brian Tracy, Buck Rogers, Jack Welch, Jack Canfield, Stephen Covey, Jim Rohn, Harvey Mackay, and too many more to list here.

Special thanks to Cat Paredi, for all of her insight, wisdom, editing skills; and for being such a wonderful partner.

I am grateful.

INTRODUCTION

When I was a younger man, I lived my life with a philosophy of, "What's in it for me?" I thought I was invincible. I was in great shape, a student of the martial arts for nine years, a top rated racquetball player. I had good friends, a great job teaching at the University of Florida. I was on top of the world.

That all changed with one sentence... *"You need to get your affairs in order, you have three months, six at the most to live."*

I sat across the desk from my oncologist as he spoke these words that shook my world, my very core. I thought he must be talking about somebody else. This couldn't be happening to me. I am too young [25 years old], I am in great shape... It can't be true!

I was diagnosed with metastasized melanoma, a very rapid form of cancer. The doctor told me that there really wasn't anything they could do for my type of cancer. He explained that once it was in your blood system, it was just a matter of time before it attacked major organs.

He asked if I would be willing to try different types of experimental treatments. In addition to chemotherapy, he wanted to inject me with tuberculosis from cows once a week, using a 24-prong needle right into my thigh. I figured I had no other options, so I said why not.

The treatment made me unbelievably ill. There were many times when I thought that death would be kinder.

At the time all this was taking place, I continued to do the best I could to live my life. My friends and family were very supportive. I had two dogs that were my best friends in the world. One was a Great Dane named Dante and the other was a German Shepherd named Zack.

Then the strangest series of events happened.

One day when I arrived home from teaching at the university, I was shocked to find only Zack in the back yard. I had an acre of fenced yard for them to run in. The fence was five feet high, the gates were locked; but Dante was not there.

I knew no one in their right mind would try to take a 185 pound dog that was in a locked fence with a German Shepherd! The only conclusion I could come to was that Dante had leaped the fence.

This was not something he had ever done before. As a matter of fact, Dante was such a good dog that if I left the gate open, he would not have wandered off.

I started a search for him. I could not find him.

Later that evening, I received a phone call from a trucker. He said that Dante had run into the road right in front of his 24 wheeler, and there was nothing he could do. He was very apologetic, and I thanked him for making the call to inform me.

Well, that night I sat there in my room crying. Questioning GOD about how he could take my best friend from me at a time when I was dying. I was angry and I was extremely upset with GOD and the world. I did not get much sleep that night.

The next morning, I was getting dressed to go to the oncologist for another round of injections when the phone rang. It was the nurse at the doctor's office. She said that the doctor needed to talk to me. I was so upset and still angry, I reacted to her and said, "What the hell does he want!" The doctor got on the phone and he was crying, I could hear it in his voice. I thought to myself, this can't be good.

Then he said those magical, wonderful words, "You don't have cancer!" He told me that he had sent my slides and blood work to the top doctor in the world for melanoma, and he verified that I was cancer free.

Well, there we were, both of us crying and laughing. We were celebrating. I thanked him for the good news and immediately picked up the phone again to call my father who lived in California.

I woke my father up. I told him I had good news and I had bad news. He wanted to know the good news first. I told him I was cancer-free. He immediately said, "How could there be any bad news after hearing this?" I told him about Dante.

My father paused. I could hear him take a deep breath and he continued, "I can't

believe what you just said to me. I have
to tell you a story".

He told me that when he was in the
army, he had a dog. Since he was the
sergeant he was able to keep the dog
with him wherever he went. One day
the dog was missing from the barracks.
He posted signs all over the base. About
two weeks later, a private returned from
a mission, saw the note and went to
tell my father the sad news. Prior to the
mission, the dog ran in front of one of
the jeeps on a rainy night and was killed.

My father wrote home to my
grandmother and told her of the loss of
his dog. She wrote back and told him
that she no longer had to worry about
him in the war. That in the village in
Austria where she grew up, they had a
belief that if a man was close to his dog,

the dog would give their life for the master.

Wow!

My father and I cried and then celebrated our pets.

Now most of you may not believe in such things. That is okay.

I believe that my dog jumped that fence for a very specific reason.

This book is not about dogs and masters. It is about the celebration of each and every day.

From that day forward, I made the decision to treat each day as a gift.

I don't know why I was given all of these extra days. I do know that I am grateful for each and every one of them.

TGIT (tig'-it) is my mantra. It is a mantra of appreciation and gratitude for every day.

This book is designed to provide you with "Food for Thought".

Open to any chapter and fill your mind with something positive rather than the negative media information you are exposed to on a daily basis.

You *do* have a choice, each and every day, to have a good day, a great day!

Every day is a gift, and the quality of your life is your gift to yourself.

Barry Gottlieb

ATTITUDE

"It's not what happens to you that determines how far you will go in life; it is how you handle what happens to you."

Zig Ziglar

Research studies indicate that 85% of the reason you get a job, keep a job, and get ahead in a job, is your attitude.

Have you heard this before? Most of us have. Yet we seem to forget how important this key characteristic of 'a Winner' is.

It is your attitude, not your aptitude, that determines your altitude.

Think about your experiences in retail stores and restaurants. If you are like me, the attitude of an employee can either make or break a deal. I will not go back to a restaurant where the food was good, but the attitude of the employee[s] was negative. It reflects on the entire experience.

Who would you choose: the doctor that says you are the one in a hundred that will survive, or the doctor [equally skilled] that says ninety-nine out of a hundred people die from this, your chances aren't very good? The choice is obvious.

Attitude *does* make a difference!

Attitudes are contagious... Is yours worth catching?

ACTION STEPS

♦ Think of someone that is a great role model. List the qualities and characteristics that make them such a positive role model. For example: they are honest, trustworthy, caring, kind, loving, have integrity. List at least twenty to thirty characteristics.

♦ Now take a pen and write next to each of these characteristics whether it is a skill "S", or an attitude "A". For example, we are taught to be honest; but honesty isn't a skill, it is an attitude. Next, go through all the characteristics you listed and identify if they are a skill or an attitude. When you are finished, you will find, just like I have in doing this exercise live in front of hundreds of people; approximately ninety percent of the characteristics get labeled with an "A" for **attitude.**

♦ On a scale of one to five, with five being excellent, how would you rate your attitude? How would your friends, your co-workers and your employees rate your attitude? Would you want to work with you... *for* you?

♦ Remember to ask yourself, "Is my attitude worth catching?"

GOALS

"A dream or wish, is the way we would like the world to be. A goal is what we intend to make happen."

Anonymous

The vast majority of people spend more time planning their vacation or a party than they do planning their lives. As a rule, they take whatever life throws at them.

Winners, on the other hand, have learned that setting goals separates them from the mediocre.

There are three types of people in this world. People that:

1. Make it happen

2. Watch it happen

3. Say, "What happened?"

People that have goals, make it happen!

ACTION STEPS

♦ Goals should be specific and clearly defined in writing.

♦ They should be written in first person, present tense and positive [as if they already exist].

♦ Identify the obstacles and challenges you will have to overcome.

♦ Then, identify the resources and people you will need to assist you in overcoming those obstacles.

♦ Establish a set of time frames: short term, intermediate, and long term.

♦ Take immediate action!

♦ Read and recite your goals every morning when you wake up, and then again prior to going asleep.

♦ Visualize your goals. See them in your mind as you recite them.

♦ Be passionate and enthusiastic regarding your goals.

♦ Only share your goals with positive people who will support your goals.

FEAR

False **E**vidence **A**ppearing **R**eal

*"Do the thing you fear, then the
death of fear is certain."*

Ralph Waldo Emerson

95% of the things we fear are never realized. They exist only in our minds. Yet most people allow their fears to control their lives.

Another term for fear is "limiting beliefs". When we replace our limiting beliefs with a new positive belief, we can change our lives for the good. A great example of changing a limiting belief was when we went from being a non-swimmer to a swimmer. The only thing that changed was our belief!

Roger Bannister was the first man to run a sub four-minute mile. Prior to this event, the experts believed that it was physically impossible for a human to do this. They believed our hearts could not stand the strain; that our lungs could not give us the capacity.

What is even more remarkable than Mr. Bannister running a sub four-minute mile is the fact that 46 days after he changed our belief that it couldn't be done; *his* record was broken! In the next two years, dozens of others ran sub four-minute miles.

Consider this... There was a time when the Earth was flat! At least, that was the belief. The world changed, when the belief changed.

What limiting beliefs are holding you back? What fears do you have that exist only in your head? What's keeping you from having the life that you deserve?

ACTION STEPS

♦ Be aware of your limiting beliefs and fears.

♦ Understand that 95% of them are not real.

♦ Replace your fears and limiting beliefs with new powerful, positive beliefs.

♦ Write them down. First person. Present tense. In the Positive.

♦ Whenever your limiting beliefs or fears surface, say aloud, "Cancel". Then immediately replace them with your new positive beliefs.

SOAR LIKE AN EAGLE

"Identify with excellence, put your name on your work, and both your work and your name will stand the test of time."

Dr. Denis Waitley

We have all heard the expression, "If it walks like a duck and quacks like a duck; chances are, it is a duck".

Take a good look at the people you associate with. You are probably just like them. Do you like what you see?

Are you reaching your full potential? Are you where you truly want to be in your life?

You have a choice. You can waddle and quack with the ducks, or you can choose to soar like an eagle. Do you want to be the prey, or do you want to soar free and see the world from a better viewpoint? Eagles fly free. Eagles fly high and have amazing vision. They are swift and decisive. They are majestic and proud.

If you want to soar with the eagles, you need to associate with eagles!

Are your friends pushing you to reach new heights, or are they keeping you down so they don't feel like they have to change?

Yes! You have a choice. You get to decide. Are you an eagle or a duck? YOU are responsible for the quality of your life.

ACTION STEPS

♦ Give yourself a reality check up.

♦ Take an inventory of your friends and acquaintances.

46

◆ Are they ducks or eagles? (Whatever your answer, the same holds true for you.)

◆ Commit to being an eagle.

◆ Surround yourself with positive role models, mentors, and friends.

◆ Read, listen and view positive books, tapes, CD's and videos.

HAPPINESS

"There is no way to happiness.
Happiness is the way."

Dr. Wayne Dyer

In his book, *"The Art of Happiness"*, the Dalai Lama states that he believes man's purpose is to be happy.

Yet, we know so many people that appear to be unhappy. Recent studies indicate that 25% of the people in this country suffer from anxiety. This is an alarming number.

The simple solution appears to be prescriptions for anti-depressants. This is not a permanent solution; it is just a band-aid that provides a temporary cover up.

There is strong evidence that shows the more control we feel we have over our lives, the happier we are.

In order to feel you have control,
you must begin with accepting total
responsibility for YOU.

Stephen Covey, renowned author says,
"Whenever you think the problem is out
there, that very thought is the problem."

Yet most people continue to look
outside themselves for the reasons they
are unhappy. They blame their spouse,
their job, the weather, and the list goes
on.

When we accept full responsibility and
take total ownership of who we are, we
gain control of our lives.

Responsibility = control = happiness!

ACTION STEPS

♦ Be aware. Notice when you are giving up responsibility. For example: You are driving to work and some careless driver cuts you off. You get angry and upset. You may even curse at them. You hold onto this rage long after they are gone. Question: Did they make you feel the way you are feeling inside? They don't even know you exist! In all likelihood, they didn't even know they cut you off. Who is really responsible for how you are feeling? **You are!** Yet, you gave up ownership and control to a total stranger.

♦ Take ownership. "I am responsible" is one of the most powerful affirmations that you can say. Stop giving control to others.

♦ Write this affirmation down.

♦ Recite it first thing in the morning when you wake up.

♦ Recite it every time you are aware you have given up control of your life to someone or something else.

♦ Recite it again every evening before you go to sleep.

♦ No excuses. Stop blaming others and circumstances "out there", and start looking at what you can do to make positive changes in your life.

Take immediate action!

SOMEDAY ISLE

"Remember, you can earn more money, but when time is spent it is gone forever."

Zig Ziglar

I have often heard it said that one of life's greatest tragedies is when someone dies at a young age. I believe an even greater tragedy would be living to one hundred, but without ever having really lived.

Someday Isle is well known to most Americans. It is a place that we dream of, we talk about, but we never seem to arrive. Someday Isle is all of those things we wanted to do in our lives. All of the places we wanted to visit. All the things we wanted to have. But we put them off because of "Someday I'll". Someday I'll try whitewater rafting. Someday I'll finish school. Someday I'll move out of this neighborhood. Someday I'll have a family. Someday I'll be somebody.

Think about it. What have you been putting off doing that you have always wanted to do, to have, to be? Ask yourself, what is keeping you from doing these things?

Do you have limiting beliefs or fears? (See the chapters on these topics.)

Are these limiting beliefs or fears real, or are they just excuses?

What if you didn't have any excuses?

What would you do?

I have read articles about terminally ill cancer patients that have formed "Adventure Clubs". These patients have been told they are going to die, some in a few months, others in several months, and a lucky few within the next 2-5 years.

These patients started adventure clubs to seek out and do everything they were afraid to do when they were "well".

They went white water rafting, sky diving, rode roller coasters, and ate spicy foods they never tried before. They visited places they always wanted to see, but never made time for.

They simply made the best out of every day they had left, without the fear or limiting beliefs.

They would tell their loved ones they loved them, every day. They didn't hold back!

I want to share a secret with you...

You already know this, but chances are you may have lost sight of it. Nobody is promised tomorrow. We are all going to die one day.

You don't need to have a terminal illness to decide you want to live each and every day to the fullest.

YOU have that choice today. You always have!

ACTION STEPS

◆ Remember: Every day is a gift, and the quality of your life is your gift to yourself.

♦ When you wake up each morning, TGIT (Thank GOD It's Today).

♦ Make a list of those things you have always wanted to do or try.

♦ Make a plan to start immediately to do them.

♦ Start your own club of people who want to live, not just exist, and do some of the activities together.

♦ Tell your loved ones you love them, every chance you get, and make the chances happen.

Celebrate life!

MENTAL FITNESS

"We first make our habits, then our habits make us."

Dr. Denis Waitley

I know if you are like most people, you make New Year's resolutions. The most common resolutions focus on changing the way you look. This is the time when most health clubs attract the majority of their members and the sale of diet related books and videos soar.

An astonishing fact is that most new health club members stop going within thirty days. Diets are started and stopped usually within the same time frame.

Why is it so hard to keep these resolutions, and others?

Why do we do what we do, when we know what we know?

The answer is HABITS.

Yes, we are creatures of habit. Your subconscious mind stores everything, forever. So how do we overcome this hurdle?

By creating new positive habits to replace, or override, the negative ones.

In order to be fit, lose weight, stop smoking, or any other resolution (or goal) you may have, you must begin by getting fit emotionally. You must begin with how you think and how you see yourself.

ACTION STEPS

♦ Start by getting mentally fit.

- ◆ Write your goals down.

- ◆ Write them in first person, present tense, and positive. For example: "I am a lean, fit, muscular 180 pounds" or "My lungs are healthy, open and clear."

- ◆ Read your goals every morning when you first get up, and then again as you prepare for bed.

- ◆ Recite them aloud, with passion and enthusiasm.

- ◆ Visualize them as if they already exist.

- ◆ Everything begins with a **thought.**

- ◆ Our thoughts become our **actions.**

◆ Our actions done repeatedly become our **habits.**

◆ All of our habits create our **character.**

If there is something we would like to change about our character, we must begin by changing the way we think.

KAIZEN

A Mantra for Happiness

"A picture may be worth a thousand words, but a wise man is worth a thousand pictures."

Fred Bishop

Kaizen (ky-zen') means *"continuous learning and growth"*.

Research studies indicate that there is a direct correlation between how much a person reads and the level of success and happiness they achieve. Are you aware that the average American reads approximately one book each year?

How many books did you read this past year?

Most people make the excuse that they don't have time. Their schedules are so busy that they just can't make the time to read.

Life is all about the choices we make!

If you made the choice to get up fifteen minutes earlier, five days a week, and you read something educational, inspirational, motivational or spiritual; you would literally change your life. At the end of the year, you would have successfully read thirteen books.

Imagine that!

You would be making a choice to make things happen in your life, rather than watch things happen. You would be in an elite group of people.

Find a mentor.

Kodak has a famous saying, "*A picture is worth a thousand words*". I remember hearing this slogan one day with my dad. He turned to me and said, *"Son, a*

wise man is worth a thousand pictures."
He was right!

In this era of technology, we have access to the greatest mentors and teachers of all time, both present and past.

If you are like most people, you have a twenty to thirty minute commute to your job every morning. Why not choose to utilize this time and listen to one of these remarkable mentors? Books on CD are available in every major bookstore, or you may purchase them online.

Imagine having mentors like Sam Walton, Jack Welch, Steven Covey, and many others available to coach you. Wow, what an amazing way to start your day.

In addition to books and CD's, make a commitment to attend at least one seminar every year.

Remember, a wise man or woman is worth a thousand pictures. Seek out and find mentors that will help you grow.

ACTION STEPS

♦ Make Kaizen your mantra.

♦ Read or listen to a book for fifteen minutes every day.

♦ Find a mentor, or two.

♦ Attend seminars; get a friend to join you.

♦ Share what you learn with others. When you teach, you become the student.

♦ Take immediate action with the knowledge you have acquired.

♦ Make learning fun and exciting.

COMMUNICATION

"Truth is never afraid of question."

Fred Bishop

A survey of Fortune 100 Chief Executive Officers revealed that the number one reason they attributed to the success of their company is excellent communication.

What is the communication like in your company? With your family? With your friends?

Let's start with the basics. Did you know that the average person only remembers approximately ten percent of what they hear? Yet most of us feel we are providing excellent communication by "telling" someone what we want them to know or do. How often do you find people not doing the things you asked them to do? Do you believe they are ignoring your request intentionally? The answer is, they simply didn't remember what you asked them to do.

We remember approximately twenty-five percent of what we see. If we combine auditory with visual, we can increase retention to over sixty percent.

Add repetition to the formula, and you can increase retention to almost ninety percent.

Listening is a key factor in effective communication. GOD gave us two ears and one mouth. We should use them in direct proportion.

This simple rule, when followed, will enhance the effectiveness of your overall communication skills.

Most people are too busy interrupting someone, mid-sentence, because they want to express their opinion instead of hearing the person out. We need to practice being a good listener. The benefits are huge. First, we are letting the other person know we respect them. Second, we will grasp their entire thought process.

Next, be an active listener. This means that after you have heard them out, play back what you heard them say. This will make them feel like you really heard them and that you care. Plus, it will allow you the opportunity to make sure you got it "right".

When speaking, choose your words wisely and with care. Don't rush to get your point across. Say what you want to happen rather than what you don't want to happen. For example, "Remember to buy milk" rather than, "Don't forget the milk." Why would you want to tell someone the opposite of what you want them to do? Our subconscious mind will not accept a "negative". It hears, "Forget the milk"!

ACTION STEPS

♦ Think before you speak.

♦ Listen respectfully.

♦ Don't interrupt.

♦ Practice active listening.

♦ Remember to write notes for people in addition to telling them. This will increase the likelihood of them remembering.

♦ Remember, repetition is a powerful learning tool.

♦ Speak and write clearly.

♦ Speak and write with confidence.

DAILY MENU

"The best way to prepare for life is to begin to live."

Elbert Hubbard

Every day is a gift.

Is this statement something that you can relate to, or do you take each day for granted like most people? When you start your day, are you planning on having a great day, or are you settling for whatever that day may turn out to be?

Are you aware that you actually have a choice? Yes, that's right; you have a choice whether you are going to have a good day or a bad day.

You may not be able to control the events that occur during the day, especially those events that are unexpected and challenging. But, you definitely have a choice whether you are going to allow these events to ruin your day, and how are you going to face these challenges.

Most people will dwell on the challenges and allow them to affect them. They will wallow in their misfortune.

Winners on the other hand, will look for solutions and take positive action.

We all face challenges every day. Winners deal with these challenges in a positive way. Losers see them as problems.

ACTION STEPS

♦ Create the winning habit of choosing to have a great day, every day!

♦ When you first get up each morning, TGIT.

♦ Pretend you are handed a menu. On one side of the menu is a happy face and it reads, "Great Day". On the other side of the menu it reads, "Bad Day".

♦ Choose GREAT DAY!

♦ Resolve that when you are faced with unexpected challenges, you are going accept them and immediately find solutions.

♦ Take immediate action!

♦ Avoid replaying the challenge of bad news. Pre-Play what you want to happen.

◆ Move forward.

Remember... Every day is a gift, and the quality of your life is your gift to yourself.

LIMITING BELIEFS

"One who fears failure limits his activities. Failure is only the opportunity to more intelligently begin again."

Henry Ford

Limiting Beliefs...

We all have them, yet most of us are unaware that they exist. They are keeping us from having the life we deserve. They come in all shapes and sizes. They are often masked by denial and deflection. But, they are there. Most of them are not real, except in our own minds.

A few of us are fortunate. We are not afraid to face them. This is the first and most important step toward making changes that will have a powerful impact on our lives and our overall well being.

What are *your* limiting beliefs?

Do you think you are: not smart enough, not tough enough, not pretty enough, too old, too fat, too thin? What are you afraid of; the dark, water, snakes, failure, success, public speaking, changing jobs, a commitment, or something else?

Here are some action steps that will assist you in overcoming your limiting beliefs.

ACTION STEPS

♦ Identify your top three to five limiting beliefs.

♦ Write each one on a separate sheet of paper.

♦ Then, on another sheet of paper, write a new positive belief to replace the limiting belief.

♦ Often, this is the opposite of the limiting belief. Better stated, it is what you are "for" rather than what you are "against". For example, a limiting belief might be stated as, "I am overweight." Change that to your new, positive belief, "I am a lean, healthy, fit and beautiful woman."

♦ Your new positive belief should be written in first person, present tense, and in the positive; as if it already exists.

♦ Close your eyes and visualize your new positive belief.

♦ Recite it aloud with passion and enthusiasm.

♦ See it as if it already exists.

◆ Get excited!

◆ Now, take your old negative limiting belief, tear it up and throw it away. As you do this, recite, "I let it go." Immediately visualize your new positive belief and recite it again with passion and enthusiasm.

◆ Take your time. Really get into it.

◆ The more you visual you are and the more passionate you are, the stronger the picture becomes in your subconscious mind.

◆ For the next thirty days, recite and visualize your new positive beliefs.

♦ Do this when you first wake up and again before you go to sleep, every day.

♦ If your old beliefs try to resurface, and they usually do, say aloud, "Cancel!" and immediately replace that thought with your new positive belief.

♦ This requires discipline.

♦ You must be committed and bold!

GRATITUDE

"Develop an attitude of gratitude."

Brian Tracy

Many years ago, I was sitting in a seminar given by Dr. Norman Vincent Peale, author of the "Power of Positive Thinking", when a man several rows in front of me stood up to make a comment at the end of the seminar.

The man said to Dr. Peale, "All this positive thinking stuff may work for some people, but you have no idea what my problems are." The man continued, "My problems are overwhelming, and you don't realize how tough I have it. I don't have just one problem. I have countless problems." Dr. Peale let the man finish venting and then he asked the man if he would like to go with him to visit a place with a population of over twenty thousand people, where not one person had a problem.

The man got very excited and said, "I would like to go there." Dr. Peale informed the man that it was just a thirty-minute drive to the Woodlawn Cemetery, and he would be happy to take him there after the seminar was over.

The rewards in life are not given for identifying the problems. They are given for finding the solutions.

Be solution oriented! The most powerful ally in overcoming your problems is changing your focus. When you focus on your problems, they tend to get bigger and they seem to multiply.

ACTION STEPS

♦ Make a written list of all of those things you have in your life for which you should be grateful.

♦ Focus on the good that is already present.

♦ Focus on the abundance that you have in your life. That's right, the abundance.

♦ Look for it. You will find it! The fact that you are sitting there reading this is a starting point for those of you who say you have nothing to be grateful for:

  o You have the gift of vision

  o You can read

- o   You have a computer

- o   You have manual dexterity

- o   Someone cares about you

- o   You have a roof overhead

- o   You are breathing

♦ This is just a small example of how we take things for granted.

♦ I once had a mentor say to me, "If you don't believe every day is a gift, try missing one."

♦ Change your focus.

POSITIVE SELF DISCIPLINE

"No man is free who is not master of himself."

Epictetus

Every year, Americans spend billions, yes, *billions* of dollars trying to improve themselves.

They go to seminars, read books, and listen to motivational CD's that are filled with powerful, life changing lessons.

Yet, the vast majority of these people show no discernible changes in their lives. Oh, they get excited for a brief period of time. But then they fall back to the same routine and patterns they have always had.

But, there are those few select individuals who change dramatically. They achieve the levels of happiness

and success they were looking
for.

How did they accomplish this? What
is different about them? They read the
same books. They attended the same
seminars. They listened to the same
CD's.

What is the missing ingredient that
enabled them to achieve their desired
goals?

What is keeping you from having the life
that you deserve? The answer is really
quite simple.

The **key** is positive self-discipline!

Positive Self Discipline ("PSD") is the
key that unlocks the door and starts the
engine for the life you deserve. Without

this key (PSD), it is just theory. You must take action, consistently, in order to create permanent change.

Don't get me wrong. I am a huge fan of positive thinking and of positive attitude. I give seminars on these two topics all the time. But they alone are not enough. You must take consistent action with PSD in order to create new, winning habits.

Imagine if you will, meeting Tiger Woods. In this meeting, Tiger explains to you how to become a golf superstar. He shares with you all the skills and drills that have made him the best in the game. This alone will not change your game, though. I am sure you will be excited and enthusiastic. But in order to create lasting change, you must develop PSD. You must practice consistently what you have learned. You must take action.

This holds true in your personal life as well. The books and seminars are great. Now commit to taking consistent action using Positive Self Discipline.

TIME MANAGEMENT

"Lack of direction, not lack of time, is the problem. We all have twenty-four hour days."

Zig Ziglar

How would you like to get more accomplished and feel more successful on a regular basis? "Time management" is your answer.

Are you aware that most people have very poor or no time management skills?

If you are one of these people, don't feel bad; most people have never been taught these skills. As a matter of fact, research tells us that almost 80% of Americans have poor time management skills. I am going to share with you my *"Brilliant on the Basics"* strategies for improving your time management skills.

ACTION STEPS

♦ To begin with, you will need the following tools: A pencil or pen and a stick 'em note pad.

♦ Step One: Before you go to bed at night, make a list of one to five things that are your priorities for the next day. Remember, the maximum amount you may list is five things.

♦ Step Two: Review your list and place them in order (top priority first). Special Note: Most people get caught in the trap of doing the things that are urgent, rather than doing the things that are important. Stay focused on your priorities.

◆ Step Three: Read your list prior to going to sleep. Try to visualize the way you would like your day to go tomorrow. By doing this, your subconscious mind will actually work on these tasks while you are sleeping. It will think of ways to overcome any obstacles you may encounter the next day.

◆ Step Four: When you wake up in the morning you will have the option to change anything on your list, in case you overlooked something that is a more important priority.

◆ Finally, you have hit the ground running. You are way ahead of most people. Focus on your top priority and get it done. Do not allow anything to distract you from your mission. Scratch it off your list when completed, and move on to the next priority, and so on.

♦ Do not add to your list until you have completed all of your priorities.

YOUR
WORD

"One lie ruins a thousand truths."

Ghanaian Proverb

"Do I have your word?"

Have you read the book, *"The Four Agreements"*, by Don Miguel Ruiz?

I highly recommend this book to all of you. In his book, the author shares four very simple yet powerful agreements that, if followed on a consistent basis, will change your life forever.

The first of the four agreements is, "Be impeccable with your word. Speak with integrity. Say only what you mean. Avoid using the word to speak against yourself or to gossip about others. Use the power of your word in the direction of truth and love."

This is the focus of this chapter; keeping your agreements and your word.

There was a time when a person's word was his bond. But, today it seems that agreements are given too often without a real commitment to honoring that agreement.

Take a good look at yourself. Are you a person of integrity? Do you honor your word?

When we do not live up to our agreements, we not only lose the trust, credibility and faith of others, we learn to distrust ourselves. Our integrity and self-concept suffer.

Every agreement you make, ultimately, is with yourself.

When you realize how important your integrity and self-concept are, you will think twice before making an agreement that you do not intend to keep.

Those casual agreements we agree to, like meeting somebody after work, or picking something up for a friend, or calling someone later. These may seem like innocent agreements, but they are commitments! When we don't keep our word, we are saying more about who we are than we may realize.

When you keep your word, you speak volumes about the person you truly are. You earn the respect and trust of others.

Here are some action steps you can take on making and keeping your agreements.

ACTION STEPS

◆ Pause before you give your word and say you are going to do something. Make sure it is something you intend to do.

◆ Write down your commitments. Use a day planner or calendar.

◆ If you can't keep an agreement, let the other person know immediately.

◆ Learn to say "No" more often.

◆ Remember, actions speak louder than words.

LISTEN

"The true way to soften one's troubles is to solace those of others."

Madame De Maintenon

"The deepest hunger of the human soul is to be understood. The deepest hunger in the human body is for air. If you can listen to another person, in depth, until they feel understood, it is the equivalent of giving them air."

Stephen Covey

One of the greatest skills we can master is the art of listening. When we listen to another person we let them know that we value them; that we care about them and what they have to say. We show them that we respect them.

Are you a good listener? Do you truly listen to others when they are speaking with you? Or are you caught up in thinking about what you are going to say back to them? Do you allow them to finish their thoughts and sentences, or are you interrupting them mid-sentence to insert your opinions?

When we interrupt people, we are in essence telling them that we are ignoring what they have to say. We are ignoring *them*. We are sending them a message that we don't care! This is the equivalent of an emotional slap in the face. Most of us are not even aware that we do this.

GOD gave us two ears and one mouth. We need to use them in direct proportion. This simple rule, if followed, will lead to success in all kinds of relationships, both personal and professional.

The more you listen and the better you listen; the more people will like you, trust you and want to be associated with you. Great listeners are admired and respected. They tend to be winners. They end up at the top of their field. They have great personal relationships.

ACTION STEPS

♦ Listen attentively and respectfully. Hear the person out.

♦ Avoid interrupting.

♦ Play back to them what you heard them say. This is called "active listening". This let's them know that you got it; that you understood.

◆ Pause before you respond. Gather your thoughts.

◆ Practice the art of being a great listener and you will show respect, and be respected.

THE EXTRA MILE

"It is never crowded along the extra mile."

Wayne Dyer

When I first started in business thirty years ago, I was taught a lesson that would prove to be one of the major keys to my success. The lesson was to do more than you are paid to do.

It seemed so simple, yet I noticed that most people did not believe in or follow this simple philosophy.

On the contrary, I noticed that most people had the exact opposite philosophy. I would hear people say things like, "That's not what they pay me to do", or "If they paid me more, I would do more."

I noticed that these were the same people that were always complaining about all the things that were wrong with the company or with their boss. They would blame their lack of success on someone or something outside of themselves.

In the late '80's I attended a three-day seminar, "The Successful Life Course". The seminar was presented by former congressmen Ed Foreman and his team. One of the key things that I learned from this course was, "Winners develop the habit of doing the things that losers don't like to do." The lesson was reinforced. It was clear, simple and true!

The harder you work, the luckier you get.

Author Wayne Dyer said, "It is never crowded along the extra mile."

Are you consistently someone who goes the extra mile?

It is a fact that most successful people do more. They are the ones that arrive early and stay late. They are the ones that stand above the rest. They are the winners, and they reap the rewards.

They are not there because they are smarter or more gifted. They are there because they work harder.

What can you expect if you adopt this philosophy of success? When you give more than expected, you are more likely to receive recognition for a job well done along with bonuses, raises, and probably promotions.

You will never have to worry about job security. You will create the inner characteristics of a winner. You will be well respected by your peers and by your employer.

The philosophy is easy to understand. The challenge is accepting full responsibility for yourself and for the choices you make.

Winners make it happen!

THE
BENEFITS
OF
FAILURE

*"My great concern is not whether
you have failed, but whether you
are content with your failure."*

Abraham Lincoln

Yes, that's right, there are many benefits associated with failure. Most of us have never stopped to realize and appreciate the amazing and marvelous things that we have in our lives every day, thanks to those unflappable men and women who were not concerned about failure.

Look around you. Are you aware that most of the gadgets, appliances, tools, medicines, and luxuries that we have today, were created by individuals who chose not to give up? They accepted failure as part of the learning process to achieve their objectives.

One of the greatest inventors of our time, Thomas Edison, was laughed at by his colleagues and ridiculed by the press during his attempt to bring us the electric light bulb. Edison's famous quote was, "I did not fail five thousand times to create the filament, I successfully identified five thousand ways not to."

Can you imagine the Wright Bothers giving up after one try? Where would aviation be today if they did not persist?

How about Jonas Salk, Madame Curie, and countless other famous doctors that gave us miracle drugs and cures?

Do you know the value of never giving up?

Are you aware that the greatest basketball player of all time, Michael Jordan, didn't start on his high school team? Did you know that Albert Einstein didn't pass his college entrance exam the first time?

The list goes on and on. So many of the people that we have come to recognize and admire had a similar view and belief.

They did not fear failure!

On the contrary, they recognized that in order to accomplish anything new or to achieve something they had not been able to do; they had to be willing to take chances. They had to be willing to accept failure and rise above it.

Eleanor Roosevelt once said, "You can gain strength, courage and confidence by every experience in which you really stop to look fear in the face. You must do the thing you think you cannot do".

What is holding you back? What is keeping you from achieving the life that you deserve? Are you willing to face your failures, learn from them, and try one more time?

I encourage you and challenge you to be bold!

YOUR MARKET VALUE

"A wise man will make more opportunities than he finds."

Sir Francis Bacon

When I gave up my tenure at the University of Florida to start a career in business, I realized how ill prepared I was for this new path I had chosen. Nobody taught me the do's and don'ts of business. Sure, I had taken courses during my ten years in college, but those courses did very little to prepare me for the real world.

I realized that I needed some practical advice from people that were actually in the trenches. From people who were living the experience, not just teaching it.

I wanted to learn from the best, from the winners, from the people who were at the top of their field.

But where do you find these people, the ones with experience and a proven track record?

The answer was simple: Books, tapes, videos and seminars.

I found out that I could tap into the knowledge of some of the greatest leaders from the past and the present. Imagine having access to people like Francis Buck Rogers from I.B.M., Sam Walton from Wal-Mart, Jack Welch from GE, and many, many more.

How powerful. How inspiring.

People that read more, listen to CD's and attend seminars, earn more and are more successful.

The average American reads approximately one book a year.

What was the last book that you read that was directly related to helping you be more successful? When did you attend your last seminar? What CD program are you listening to as you drive to work each morning?

This is what winners do on a consistent basis.

ACTION STEPS

♦ Get up 15 minutes earlier and read. Do this 5 days a week and by the end of the year you will have read 13 books!

◆ Attend at least one seminar a year.

◆ Listen to CD's on the way to work that inspire, educate and empower you.

◆ Send me an email and I will gladly supply you with my *"Top Ten"* list of books/CD's.

NOW

"The NOW is a magical place where you are uniquely capable of being so involved that there is no room for any unhappy or debilitating thoughts."

Dr. Wayne Dyer

I remember back when I was a student at the University of Florida, I was introduced for the first time to the concept of "living in the now". A friend had invited me to go hear a lecture by Babba Ram Das, the author of "Be Here Now".

The lecture was intriguing, to say the least. It had a huge impact on my way of thinking. The concept was great. The ideology of being able to live in the present, to savor each and every moment; to truly enjoy being who we are and where we are and what we are doing, right now! Wow, that was so powerful! But it was not that easy. After all, I was told that I had to plan for the future. I was taught that I had to worry about the consequences of things that could go wrong. It seemed that everything in our society, in our culture, was completely opposite of living in the now.

How do you live your life? Do you live in the now, or do you live in the past and future?

When was the last time you chose to sit and watch a sunrise or sunset? When was the last time you watched the flow of a stream or the flight of a butterfly? When was the last time you held your partner's hand and the rest of the world disappeared?

The GIFT of NOW!

I recently coached a friend of mine that just had his cancerous thyroid removed and he was waiting for the prognosis from his doctor. In our conversation he said to me, "I never realized how blue the sky was." His comment made me pause and reflect on how many things we take for granted. We are so busy worrying about the future, that we don't make the time to appreciate the present.

If you ever watch young children playing, you will realize that they are living completely in the now. They aren't worried about the past, or the future. They are living and enjoying NOW. We were those children. Those children are still inside us. We just need to keep the child inside us alive. We need to live in the now. We need to see how blue the sky really is.

Remember, nobody is promised tomorrow. This is not a dress rehearsal.

Open your eyes. Open your ears. Open your heart! Seize the day. Seize the moment! Remember... Every day is a gift, and the quality of your life is your gift to yourself.

FIGHT, FLIGHT OR FREEZE

"In any moment of decision the best thing you can do is the right thing, the next best thing is the wrong thing, and the worst thing you can do is nothing."

Theodore Roosevelt

When faced with danger, most people react in one of two ways. They either flee from the danger or they stand their ground and fight. This has come to be known as "the fight or flight reaction".

Over time, I have come to recognize that there is another reaction to danger; to freeze!

Like a deer caught in the headlights of a car, in this instance we do nothing. We don't flee and we don't fight. We are paralyzed by our fear, by the danger; and we freeze.

Of the three reactions to danger, I am convinced that the worse choice is to freeze.

Some of the saddest situations I have encountered have been clients or friends that are stuck (i.e., frozen) in abusive relationships. Too often, these people are so afraid that they remain in a work place or a personal relationship where there is absolutely no respect. There is constant and harmful verbal, and sometimes even physical, abuse.

They recognize what is going on, but they are too afraid to take action to free themselves from their situation.

If you are in a work situation where you feel you are harassed or verbally abused on a regular basis, then you must take immediate action. Go to the head of Human Resources and file a written complaint. If there is no HR department, then go to a higher level of management.

If you are in a personal relationship where you feel you are not being treated with respect and you feel paralyzed and afraid to leave; seek professional help.

There are people who can help you. You are worthy. You *can* make it on your own. You *do* have a choice.

Stop being a victim!

This is the one chance we get at this life. Why would you want to spend it with someone or in a job that doesn't respect you, value you, and encourage you?

"Come to the edge," He said.

They said, "We are afraid."

"Come to the edge," He said.

They came.

He pushed them, and they flew!

Guillaume Apollinaire

MEDITATION

*"You must be the change you
wish to see in the world."*

Mahatma Ghandi

If there was a way for you to be more relaxed, have less tension and anxiety, and feel more rested and full of energy; would you want to know about it?

What if I told you it only requires twenty minutes twice a day, slows the aging process, and it will cost you absolutely nothing?

Well, here is the answer you seek:

Meditation

I know that most of you have heard about meditation. Some of you may even have tried it at one time or another in your lives. But, most people have never attempted to meditate, mostly because of their misconception of what meditation is.

I often hear people say they can't imagine blocking everything from their mind (you don't have to), or that meditation requires too much training or discipline.

Here's an interesting observation: Most of you meditate and don't even realize it. For some of us it happens when we are sitting in a warm tub, or listening to music that takes us away, or staring at a candle or into the fireplace, or listening to the sound of the ocean or the rain.

Science has proven that there are positive benefits to regular meditation. Here are some simple action steps that will guide you through your meditation.

ACTION STEPS

- ◆ Find a quiet place.

- ◆ Ask not to be disturbed.

- ◆ Turn off your phone.

- ◆ Sit comfortably, with good posture.

- ◆ Choose a soothing word, like love, hope, peace, or a child's name.

- ◆ Close your eyes.

- ◆ Take three slow, deep breaths. Breathe in through your nose; fill your stomach, then your chest, and breathe out through your mouth.

◆ Now, breathe normally. As you do, say your soothing word aloud with each breath.

◆ After a minute, say the word in your mind and continue repeating it for 20 minutes.

◆ If you find your mind has wandered off, just relax and gently come back to your word.

WORRY

*"Whatever you have to have,
owns you."*

Dr. Wayne Dyer

Many years ago, I was on a commercial airline "puddle jumper" from Scranton to Philadelphia. There were eight seats and we shared the cabin with the pilot and co-pilot. To make matters worse, the weather looked like something out of the Wizard of Oz. The flight was bumpy and filled with sudden drops. I was very nervous, no, make that scared!

As we approached Philadelphia, things got worse. The pilot informed us that the weather was so bad we would not be able to land until things improved.

So there I was, white knuckled, holding onto my seat for dear life. I found myself staring out the window into a solid sheet of grey clouds. I was truly afraid. I sat there looking for BIG planes to come plowing into us; as if my knowing would change anything.

This went on for thirty minutes. My anxiety level was off the charts. I was so worried about all the scenarios that might occur. The fear and anxiety grew worse and worse.

Then, out of nowhere a story that I heard when I was in an Eastern Philosophy class popped into my mind.

The story was about a monk that lived in a monastery that sat on a bluff three thousand feet above the valley. Every day, the monk would go for a walk along the edge of the bluff.

One day, a hungry tiger came out of the woods and saw the monk. He started moving toward the monk.

The monk spotted the approaching tiger. He knew the tiger intended to eat him. Behind him was the valley below. In front of him was the hungry tiger.

He noticed a cherry tree growing out of the side of the bluff, about ten feet below the edge. The monk dropped down to the tree. There he sat, a hungry tiger and certain death above him, the valley floor and certain death below him. What did the monk do?

He ate and enjoyed the cherries!

LESSONS FROM THE STORY

♦ Worry will not change the outcome.

♦ Choose to live in the now.

◆ Live life to the fullest.

◆ Make the best of every situation.

◆ Look for the "good".

◆ Celebrate your life.

SUCCESS VERSUS LUCK

"It's hard to beat a person who never gives up."

Babe Ruth

Are successful people just lucky?

I remember as a little boy watching an interview on television. Gary Player, one of the greatest golfers of his time, was answering a reporter's questions. The reporter made the comment that Mr. Player was one of the luckiest golfers on the PGA Tour. Gary Player immediately responded by saying, "The harder I try, the luckier I get!"

Have you ever noticed how people in general tend to credit other people's success to luck? Do you believe this is true, or do you believe what Gary Player said?

My experience has led me to believe that success is an outcome of effort and hard work, not luck.

Thirty years ago I read a book by the CEO of ITT, Harold Geneen. The one major key to success that I walked away with after reading the book was, "Do more than you are paid to do."

In my thirty years in business, I have found that most employees do not have this attitude. I noticed that most employees adopted an attitude of, "If they paid me more, I would do more" or "That's not my job, they don't pay me to do that".

Stop waiting to win the lottery. Did you know that recent studies indicate that 68% of lottery winners, after three years, are in a worse financial position than before they won the lottery?

Take action today to create the success and happiness you deserve. Stop waiting for "Lady Luck" to knock on your door!

ACTION STEPS

- ◆ Believe and act like you and you alone are 100% responsible for YOU.

- ◆ Learn to give up the excuses.

- ◆ Stop blaming others for where you are in your life and for how much you earn.

♦ Take ownership of your actions, starting right now.

♦ Make hard work a habit as the condition for your success.

♦ Do more than you are paid to do.

♦ Remember: Winners develop the habit of doing the things that losers don't like to do.

BALANCE

"Time you enjoy wasting, was not wasted."

John Lennon

I received several emails from readers in response to my article on "Success". They wanted to know how to be successful at work while at the same time being a successful parent or partner. They wanted to know if you have to sacrifice one for the other.

I believe that without balance in *all* aspects of your life, you cannot be totally successful and happy.

Start by knowing, with clarity, what you really want your life to be like. What is the picture you have of yourself physically, emotionally and spiritually? What does success look like to you and your loved ones? What are your core values and beliefs? These are your foundation! They set the bar for what is right or wrong, for what is fair and unfair.

Govern yourself by these standards.

Be aware of the choices you make. Ask yourself if they are consistent with your core values and beliefs.

Remember… We teach people how to treat us. If you are out of balance by working too many hours, you and only you can change this pattern.

You have a choice!!!

WINNING RELATIONSHIPS

"You cannot be friends upon any other terms than upon the terms of equality."

Woodrow Wilson

In this day and age of instant gratification, more people are finding it increasingly harder to create long lasting, winning relationships.

Whether these relationships are at home or in the work place, it seems harder than ever to make them work.

We live in a global business culture that is built on creating lasting, positive relationships. Ask any business owner, and they will tell you there are competitive, similar products coming from all over the world. So how does a company set itself apart if the product is that similar?

By creating positive relationships!

The same should hold true in our personal relationships. So why is it that so many fail?

I am certainly not an expert on this topic. Even the experts don't seem to have the answers to this puzzle. But I do have some thoughts that might shed some light on how to create an environment where the odds tilt in your favor of making it work, and making it last.

When we first meet someone we are attracted to, we focus on all of the qualities and characteristics that we like. Over time, we stop looking at those things, and we start looking for their imperfections. A friend sent me a quote the other day that is very relevant to this. "Being happy does not mean that everything is perfect. It means that you have decided to look beyond the imperfections." We need to remember all the qualities for which we are grateful.

We need to communicate more often, and we need to be candid. Great communication is the foundation of all great relationships. Make time to talk about the relationship. Here is a simple yet powerful question that will spark great communication, "On a scale of one to ten, with ten being the best, how would you rate me as a partner?" Insist on honesty! Any score lower than a ten, immediately follow up with this question, "What would I have to do to make it a ten?"

If you are open and honest, and use this tool in a positive way to open the lines of communication, you will both have the opportunity to make your relationship grow and last.

Lastly, consider this Zen saying, *"The elm tree cannot completely grow and flourish if it is planted in the shade of the oak tree".*

TRUE ABUNDANCE

"If you want others to be happy, practice compassion. If you want to be happy, practice compassion."

The Dalai Lama

What does "True Abundance" mean to you?

According to Wikipedia, the definition of abundance is "the opposite of scarcity".

I believe true abundance is not measured by what you have; rather, it is measured by what you give.

In our culture, it seems that most people are caught up in their "need for greed". Perhaps this is why so many people struggle to find their happiness. Perhaps this is why over 25% of the people in our country suffer from anxiety. We live in a society where we are taught to judge a person based on what they have, rather than on who they are and what they contribute to society.

I was very fortunate to have met a professor that changed my whole way of thinking. I was one of those people with a "What's in it for me?' attitude when I started his class. By the end of the semester though, my philosophy and my attitude had changed. Forever! This is what I learned:

You can have anything you want in life, if you will just help enough other people get what they want.

I challenge you to focus on this philosophy for an entire month! Here are some action steps that will help you stay focused on this incredible gift.

ACTION STEPS

♦ Gratitude. Every night before you go to sleep, recite aloud at least ten things for which you are grateful.

♦ Forgive. Let go of the past. Forgive those who have hurt or angered you in the past. Stop carrying this poison around with you every day.

♦ Love. Be sure to tell those people in your life that mean so much to you that you love them and appreciate them.

♦ Donate. Go through your closets. Anything you haven't worn or used in the past year, box it or bag it and take it to a place where those who are less fortunate will benefit from your donation. Get your children involved!

◆ Praise. Make time to praise. Look for and recognize the good in others.

PERFECT
PRACTICE

"The harder I try, the luckier I get."

Gary Player

Does practice make perfect?

Most of us have heard this saying since we were little children. But the statement is not accurate. My daughter reminded me the other day of the importance of never giving up.

She said that if you miss a shot (she is a basketball player), it just means you have to go out there and practice even more.

Well, she is right about going out there to practice even more. But if you really want to improve in everything you do, you need to practice doing it the correct way.

Practicing a bad habit doesn't make it better. The key is finding and practicing the correct way to do it. The truth is: "Perfect" practice makes perfect.

ACTION STEPS

♦ Find great coaches or mentors.

♦ Take lessons from a qualified instructor.

♦ Practice what you have learned.

♦ It takes time to create new winning habits.

GROWING UP

"The sculptor produces the beautiful statue by chipping away such parts of the marble block as are not needed. It is a process of elimination."

Elbert Hubbard

If you are like most people, you may often wonder whether or not you really want to be doing what you are doing in your professional or personal life.

For many of us, we seek answers that are not always easy to find.

We look outside of ourselves at material objects as a source of validation for where we are in our lives. We measure our worth by the things we have, rather than by who we are and how we contribute to society and to mankind.

We may stay in jobs and relationships even though they are not fulfilling our inner needs.

Recognize that it is not what we are doing or who we are with. Rather, it is who we are!

Look inward... search your soul.

ACTION STEPS

♦ Most of us have lost sight of the value of doing nothing. We get caught up in the daily pace and forget to make time to unload and recharge.

♦ Create the winning habit of making time for yourself to just sit and reflect... Focus on all that you have in your life to be grateful for.

♦ Let go of your stress... relax... breathe!

RESPECT

"Whenever you judge someone else, you do not define them, you define yourself."

Stephen Covey

My father dropped out of school when he was in the eighth grade, but he managed to acquire a PhD in street smarts. He was one of my greatest mentors. One of the best lessons I learned from him was the following, "Don't judge a man by the way that he treats the president of a company; judge him by the way he treats the janitor of the company".

My Pop was right!

Everyone deserves to be treated with respect.

This should be one of the core values of your family and of your business. Respect starts with you. If you don't respect yourself, you will find it very difficult to respect others. Remember: when you command respect, people will gladly follow you. When you demand respect, they will work against you.

ACTION STEPS

♦ Praise publicly.

♦ Criticize privately.

♦ Look for the good.

♦ Catch people doing things right, and praise them for it!

♦ Let people know that you genuinely care.

♦ Separate the person from the action. Let them know it is the action that you do not approve of, not them.

♦ Be candid and sincere.

POSITIVE ROLE MODELS

"The only thing necessary for the triumph of evil is for good men to do nothing."

Edmund Burke

Wanted: Positive Role Models

Quick... Name two positive role models that your children hear about, or see on a regular basis.

How about you? Can you name two positive role models that you look up to?

What happened to the role models that we could look up to and emulate? Where have all our heroes gone?

Why is it that we allow people like Paris, Britney, OJ, Anna Nicole, and too many others to dominate the minds of our children, and us? Why is it that we are fascinated by bad role models and by bad news?

The media knows... this is what sells.

We are better than this!

There are amazing stories, about ordinary people, happening every day. We owe it to our children and to ourselves to look for, recognize, and celebrate these every day heroes and stories. It is up to us to make this happen!

ACTION STEPS

- ◆ Look for and identify positive role models in everyday life.

- ◆ Discuss them with your children and your friends.

♦ Focus on the good and the positive role models that exist, all the time.

♦ Read or watch biographies of famous role models.

♦ Stop glorifying bad role models.

♦ BE the role model you would like your children and your friends to be!

KNOWLEDGE IS POWER

"If you want to be successful and happy, you need to spend more time working on you, than you do on your job."

Jim Rohn

"Knowledge is power!"

Is this a true statement? Does knowledge really give us power?

The answer may surprise you.

Even though we have heard the statement over and over again, it is not true. Knowledge is only powerful when you use it! Think about it. If Tiger Woods spent sixty minutes teaching us the art of putting, would that make us better golfers? Only if we practiced what he taught us! If the Surgeon General told us that smoking causes cancer, would that knowledge give us power? I hope so! But only if we use it. We have access to almost unlimited information and knowledge. Yet only a small percentage of us use that knowledge to empower ourselves, and others. Enrich your life and that of others. Take your knowledge and use it for a positive purpose!

ACTION STEPS

♦ Read something inspirational, educational or spiritual every day.

♦ Attend at least one seminar every year.

♦ Teach what you learn to others. Whenever you teach, you become the student.

♦ Turn your knowledge into power by taking consistent action.

♦ Remember: Perfect practice makes perfect.

BEWARE OF NEGATRONS

"Winners develop the habit of doing the things that losers don't like to do."

Ed Foreman

Who or what is a "Negatron"?

You can find them at work, at play, at social events, or almost anywhere you go. Negatrons are people that focus on the bad, the negative, the worst of times.

They are the people that like to criticize, condemn and complain. They like to suck you into their world of apathy and mediocrity.

They do all they can to keep you from moving ahead. They are intent on keeping you down because it makes them feel better knowing they are not alone.

They follow the belief that "misery loves company".

Negatrons want you to work less, try less, and achieve less! They are this way because it makes them feel better to know there are others, just like them, that always choose the path of least resistance.

YOU are better than this!!!

ACTION STEPS

♦ Steer clear of Negatrons!

♦ Take an inventory of the people you choose to hang around with. Are they winners?

♦ Make sure your friends and colleagues build you up, rather than put you down or shut you down.

♦ Be a positive influence!

♦ Build a positive peer group that takes you to new heights.

♦ Find mentors and coaches that help you achieve your true potential.

ASSUMPTIONS

"It is better to be thought a fool, than to open one's mouth and remove all doubt."

Confucius

Most of us have heard this saying about making assumptions, "When you assume, you make an *'ass'* out of *'u'* and *'me'*." We laugh when we hear this, and we don't give it much thought.

One of the books I recommend you read is, *"The Four Agreements"*, by Don Miguel Ruiz. This is a wonderful book full of wisdom and insight.

The Third Agreement states: *"Don't make assumptions. Find the courage to ask questions and to express what you really want. Communicate with others as clearly as you can to avoid misunderstandings, sadness and drama. With just this one agreement you can completely transform your life."*

This is a very simple concept to grasp. Yet, it is difficult to practice. Why?

Because we have created, over time, the habit of assuming. We have spent most of our lives choosing to assume rather than to communicate.

You have the power to change this. Imagine how good it will feel to reduce the sadness and drama in your life, to reduce the misunderstandings and fights with friends and loved ones. You DO have a choice!

ACTION STEPS

♦ Become a great communicator.

♦ Start by being a good listener.

♦ You have two ears and one mouth; use them in direct proportion.

♦ Don't interrupt.

♦ Ask questions.

♦ Choose your words wisely.

♦ Express your feelings and your thoughts.

♦ Speak with integrity and honor.

♦ Truth is never afraid of question.

FIVE GIFTS

"Try not to become a man of success, but a man of value."

Albert Einstein

One of my favorite seminars is entitled "The Five Gifts". I love sharing this seminar because it is all about YOU giving yourself five simple gifts that will change your life forever.

Following are "The Five Gifts" in an abbreviated version.

Gift 1: Use the first hour after you wake up doing something positive. No television. No radio. No newspaper.

Gift 2: Spend thirty minutes prior to bedtime reading, listening to, or viewing something positive. No negative media or stimuli.

Gift 3: Give yourself thirty minutes to an hour every day, doing something just for you. Choose something you want to do and make it happen. No excuses!

Gift 4: Spend two to five minutes each day recognizing and acknowledging your accomplishments for the day. Pat yourself on the back!

Gift 5: Set aside five to ten minutes each day to reflect on the many things you have in your life for which you should be grateful.

Make these "gifts", habits!

EXPECTATIONS

"Seek first to understand, then to be understood."

Stephen Covey

My experience as a business/life coach and as a business owner has taught me that one of the greatest sources of frustration for leaders and managers is caused by their expectations.

We continually expect the people who work with us to do things the same way we would. To do them with the same level of intensity and passion, and to achieve the same results we would have, had we done them ourselves.

The end result is usually one of disappointment and frustration for both parties. The truth is, it is unrealistic to expect that everyone is going to do things the same way that you would. (Can you imagine if Tiger Woods was your boss and you were a golfer?)

We are all different and unique. Our experiences and education, along with our training, are all going to be at different levels. Our level of passion depends on our individual beliefs, desires, and personal histories.

Great leaders take a person from where they are and help them to grow.

Our personal relationships hold similar challenges and solutions. Celebrate the differences and find strength in them.

ACTION STEPS

- ◆ Accept people (including yourself) for who they are and what they are capable of.

- ◆ Allow them to grow and improve at a reasonable pace.

- ◆ Encourage and support them in their efforts.

- ◆ Remember, great communication is a key ingredient in improving any relationship.

- ◆ Be patient.

- ◆ Be tolerant.

- ◆ Be understanding.

◆ Be accepting.

◆ Be firm, but fair.

◆ Remember, clarity is the key!

◆ Look for the good; catch others doing things right and praise them for it.

YOUR CORE/ YOUR INTEGRITY

"Begin with the end in mind."

Stephen Covey

Having a clear picture of who you are and what you want is something that most of us don't stop to think about. We start and end our days without giving much thought to whether or not we are on the path we should be on. Most of us lead our lives without giving much thought to our true purpose or intentions. We end up trying to live the lives that the marketing and advertising companies misguide us into believing we should be living.

The end result is a society of people that are out of balance, and out of touch with what really matters to them and to others. We spend so much time trying to be something and someone other than who we really are.

Setting goals regarding where you want to get in life or who you want to be is a good start.

But, if you don't begin with *who you are and where you are*, it will be difficult for you to set a course for your desired outcome. You must begin by looking inward to understand who you are and what your core values and beliefs are. Only then will you be able to chart a course for the life that you deserve.

ACTION STEPS

♦ Give yourself a check-up from the neck up.

♦ Write down your core values and beliefs.

◆ Share them with your loved ones.

◆ Ask yourself if you are living a life consistent with these values and beliefs.

◆ Create a picture in your mind of what you want, and who you want to be in your life.

◆ Live the vision.

◆ Set clear goals that are consistent with your core values and beliefs.

◆ Celebrate your accomplishments.

◆ Acknowledge and be thankful for everything for which you feel you should be grateful.

FORGIVENESS/ LETTING GO

"GOD grant me the serenity to accept the things I cannot change; courage to change the things I can; and the wisdom to know the difference."

Reinhold Niebuhr

What are you holding on to?

We have all been there; someone or something has impacted our lives in a negative way, and we can't seem to let it go. We hold on to the event, replaying it over and over again in our minds. In doing so, we only make matters worse. This is like throwing gasoline on a fire in an attempt to put it out.

We use up vital energy by continuing to replay the event.

The fact is there are no "woulda, coulda, shoulda's". We can't change the past, no matter how hard we wish we could. All the replays in the world will not undo what has been done.

We do have a choice, though. A choice regarding how we want to deal with what happened. We have the opportunity to take our energy and apply it in a way that helps us move forward; that helps us heal.

We can learn and grow from what has happened. We can use that energy in a positive way. If we hold on to the negative, then we continue to allow that event to own part or all of us. When we make the decision to let go or forgive, we take back the power we have given away.

ACTION STEPS

♦ Make a list of the negative people or events that you are holding on to.

♦ Be aware of how these people or events make you feel.

♦ Look for the lesson that you can learn from what has happened and write it down.

♦ Recognize that replaying the event will not change what happened.

♦ Repeat aloud, "I let it go".

♦ Resolve to never let it happen again.

♦ Affirm aloud the way you want your life to be, and who you want to be.

♦ Take back control/ownership of your life.

ABOUT THE AUTHOR...

BARRY GOTTLIEB

FOUNDER: Coaching the Winner's Edge organization and coaching program

BUSINESS BUILDER: Built a $75 million international company in twenty-two years

COACH: Both a life and a business coach, with a successful practice offering counsel and guidance to individuals and major corporations

AUTHOR: "Brilliant on the Basics" which focuses on real people, real stories, and real lessons (Soon to be released)

RADIO HOST: Co-host of "The Success Show", a one-hour talk radio program broadcast weekly in South Florida

SPEAKER AND TRAINER: Inspires, coaches, and trains through programs for both large and small audiences and corporations

SALES EXPERT: Former VP of Sales for a billion dollar corporation

NEWSLETTER PUBLISHER: Founder/ Publisher of the "TGIT"(tig'-it) weekly newsletter www.tgit.org

WEBISODE HOST: Co-host of "The Insight", a half hour weekly broadcast that deals with effective change, positive thinking, holistic health, and many other topics dealing with transformation. Available at www.BocaRaton.com

PASS IT FORWARD

This book was designed to provide you with "Thought for Food". I hope you will make time every day to read something positive, and then pass it forward.

You can have everything you want in your life, if you will just help enough other people get what they want.

Remember...

Every day is a gift, and the quality of your life is your gift to yourself.

I TGIT... Do you?

With respect and gratitude,
Barry Gottlieb

WHAT OTHERS HAVE TO SAY

♦ "Our business was going through an economic and structural struggle. One month later, we started a program with Barry. We worked weekly for more than a year, and achieved more than we planned. I still carry a sense of astonishment with me when I see what our company went through. Barry's coaching was a key ingredient in this change. Structure, direction and profitability came along. Barry's business knowledge and experience combined with an enthusiastic charisma make a very effective combination that guarantee success." (William R. / President)

♦ "A man of great integrity, Barry Gottlieb imparts wisdom in a way that is both practical and relevant. I have seen him take an average group of people and turn them into an award winning team. The beauty of what he does lies in his power to motivate from the inside out. Rather than focus only on the practical, Barry focuses on the individual. This approach always leads to personal empowerment, which in turn leads to long-term team growth that is sustainable... My advice: Put Barry Gottlieb on your speed dial." (Karen G. / Producer)

♦ "Quite simply, you are the Human Whisperer." (Vicky M. /Vice President Procurement)

♦ "I just got out of a seminar with Barry Gottlieb who has become a mentor since I started working with him three years ago. I guess I chose Barry because he is "so different" from me. If I am chaos... he is Zen. If I am crazed... he is in control. After three years, I can't say that I've become like Barry. However, those who knew me in a past life might say I'm getting closer." (Bill S. /Business Development Manager)

◆ "Barry, I have to ask you, are you an angel?" (Alexandra K. /Award Winning Nationally Acclaimed Interior Designer)

◆ "Barry... I had mentioned my fear of getting on a plane to you in several conversations. I truly want to thank you for giving me advice on how to maintain a positive mental attitude and how to reverse those negative thoughts. I am very happy to tell you that last week I was finally able to overcome my fear of flying. Thank you very much. I appreciate all of your help." (Rita V. /Sales Consultant)

◆ "We are fortunate to have a company that is going forward and improving every day. You

have been an important part of our improvement and we are very grateful to you for that. We are looking forward to having a great year and consider you part of our team needed to achieve that."
(Jorge C. /President)

Made in United States
North Haven, CT
14 September 2022

24099639R00143